AF381001

Frederik Bruylant, *Dark Room*

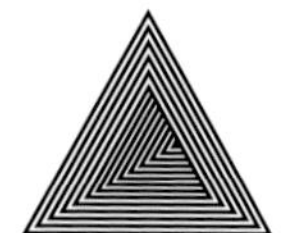

This book forms the first part of **Sleeperhold #1**.
The second is a poster bundle called « Dark Room sub ».
It was published around november 2009.
For more information and future projects visit
www.sleeperholdpublications.com.

All Photographs by **Frederik Bruylant**.
For more information visit www.frederikbruylant.com.

Sleeperhold #1 is co-hosted by **Mer Paper Kunsthalle**.
For more information visit www.merpaperkunsthalle.org.

Graphic design : Ward Heirwegh.

Printed at Cassochrome, Waregem.

ISBN : 978-90-7697-993-9
legal deposit : D/2009/1106/67

Frederik Bruylant

Dark room

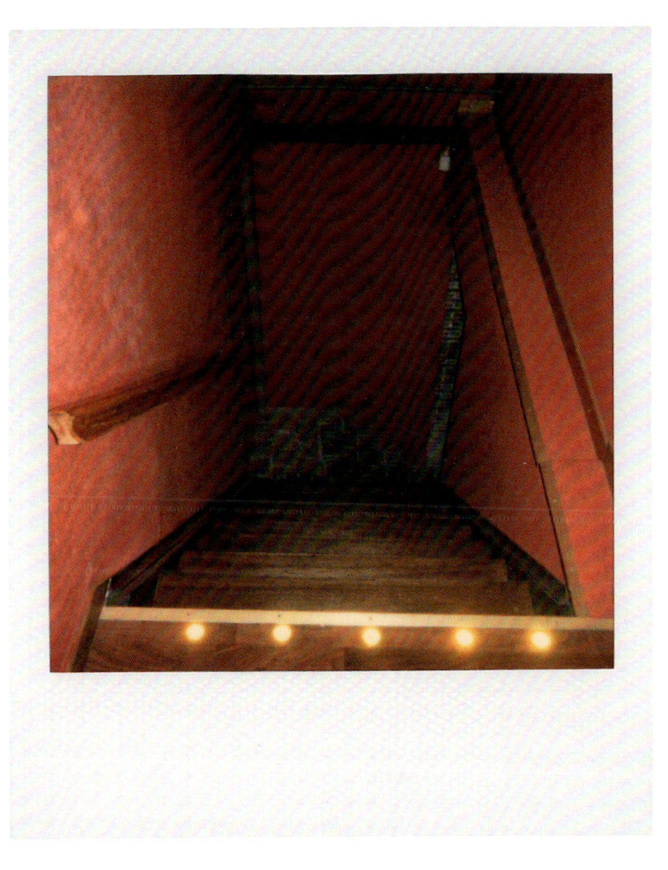

020848071
POLAROID 32

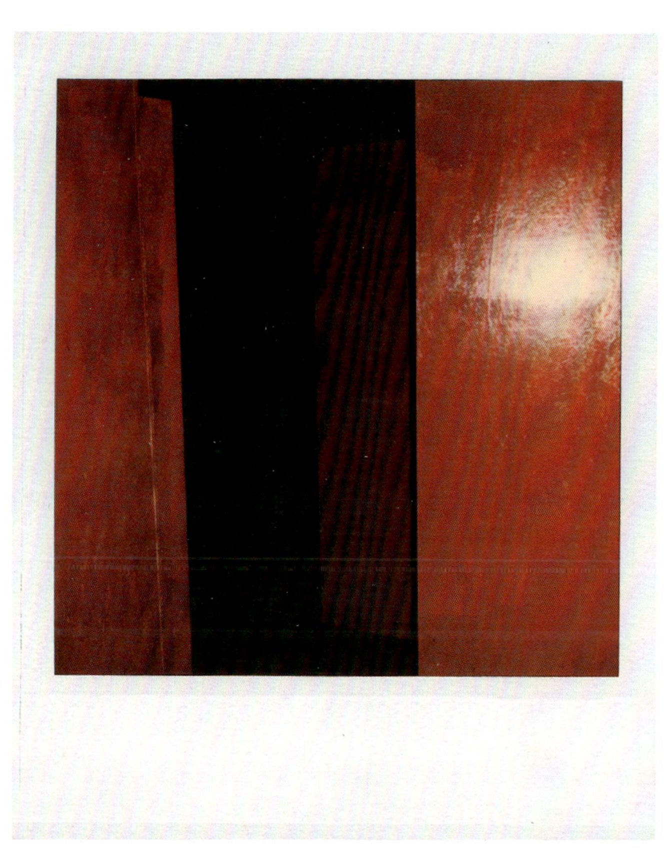

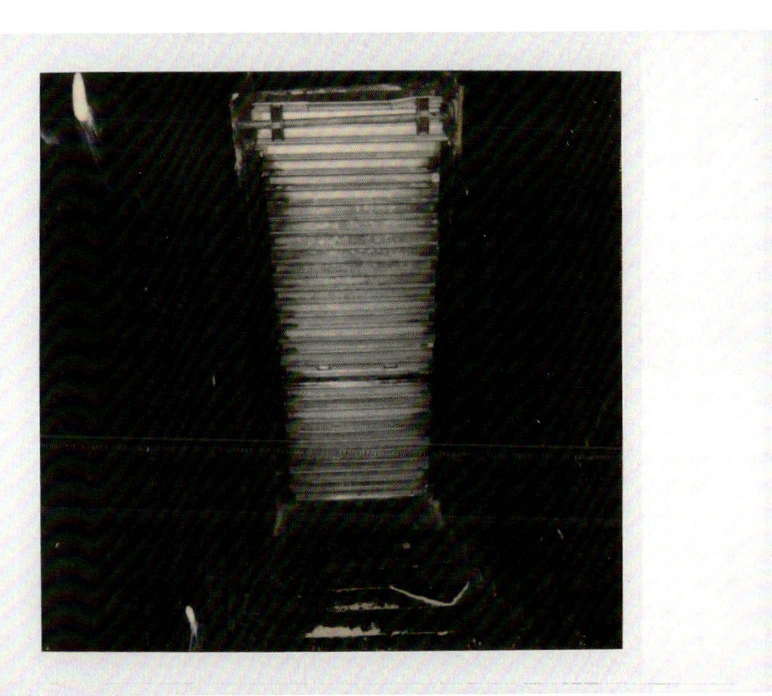

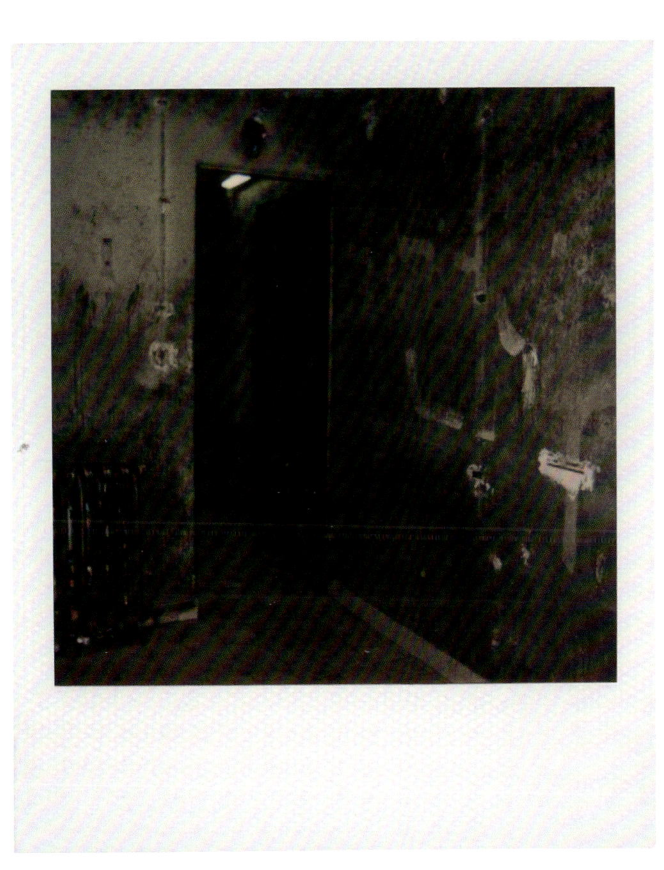

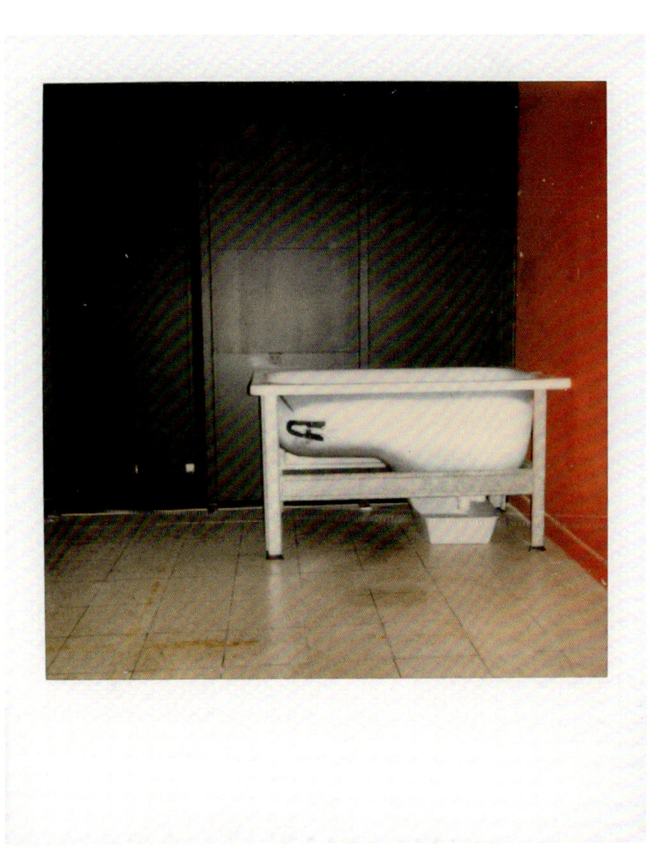

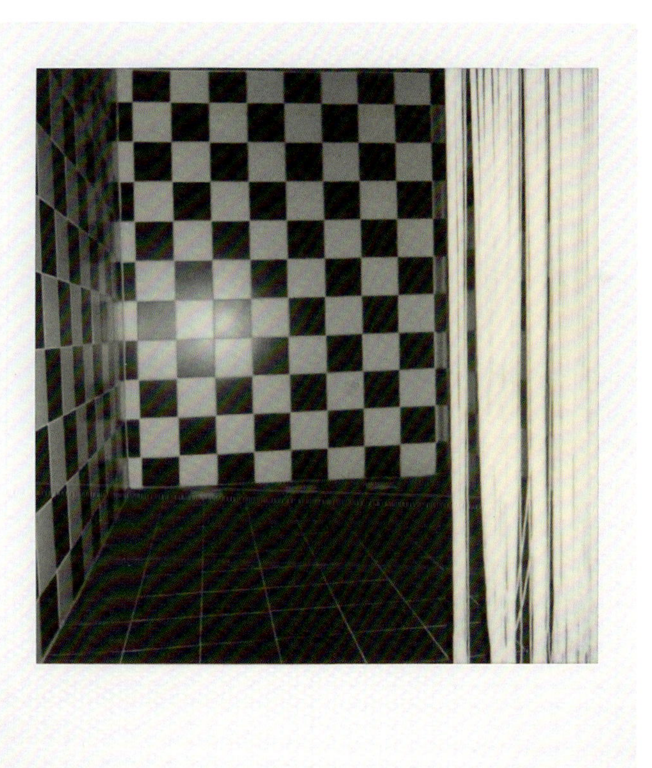

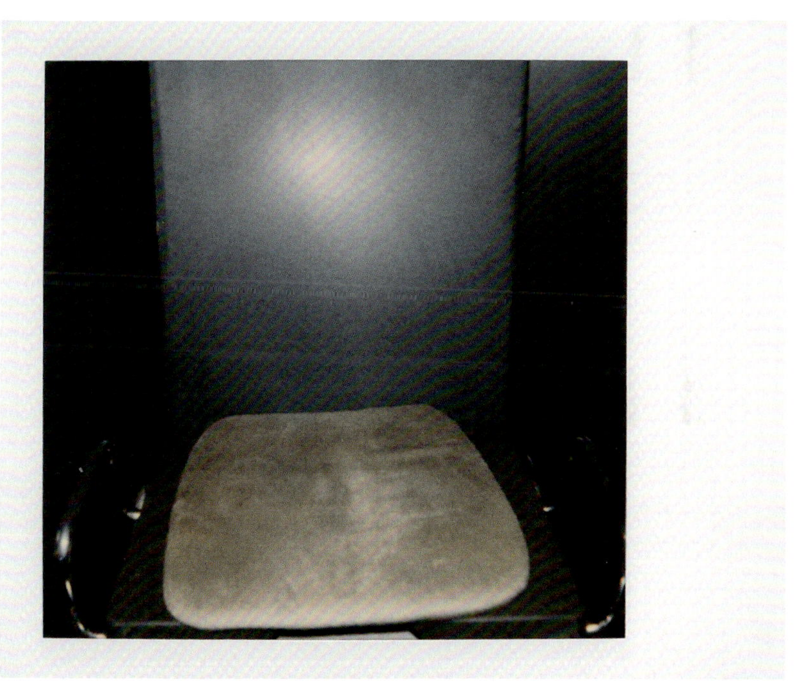

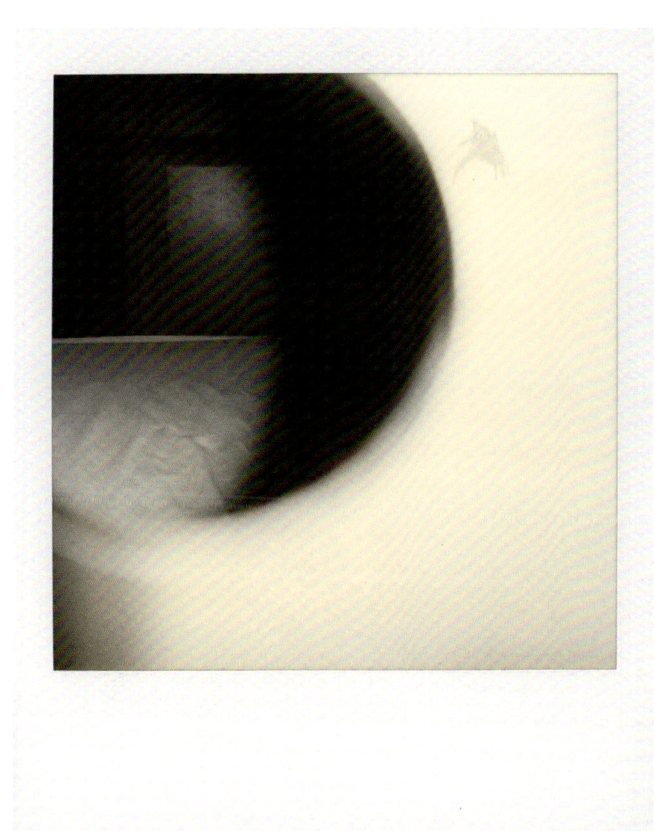

POLAROID

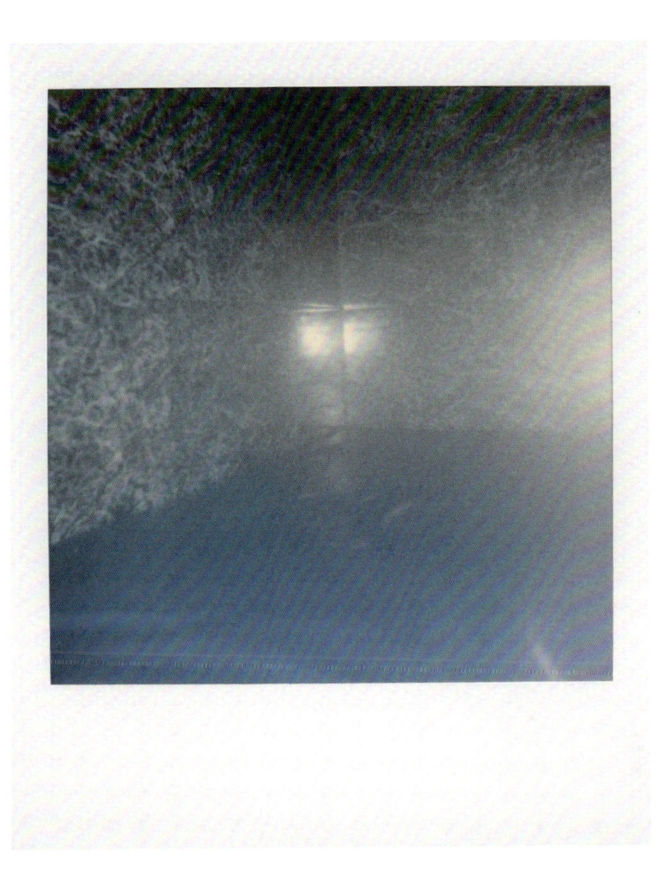

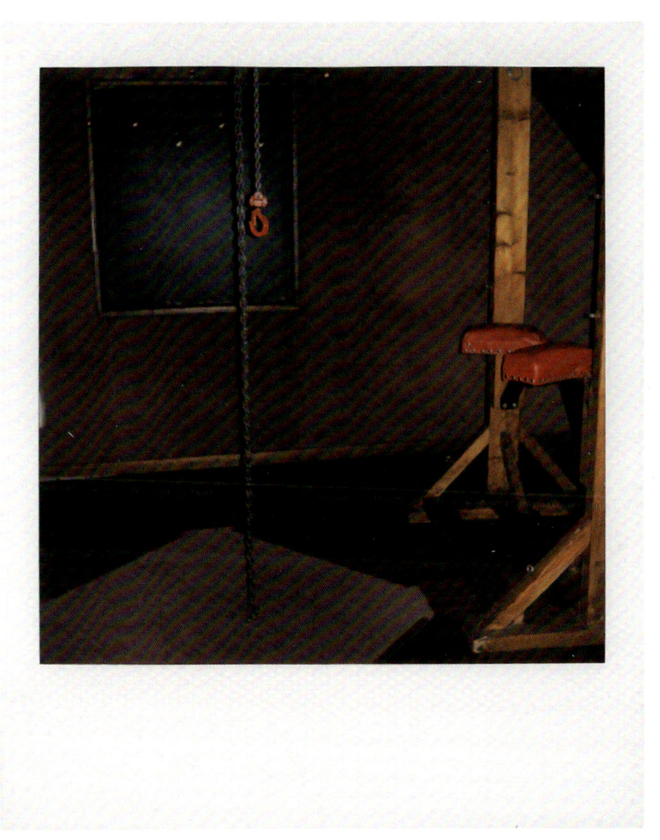

020848071
POLAROID 32

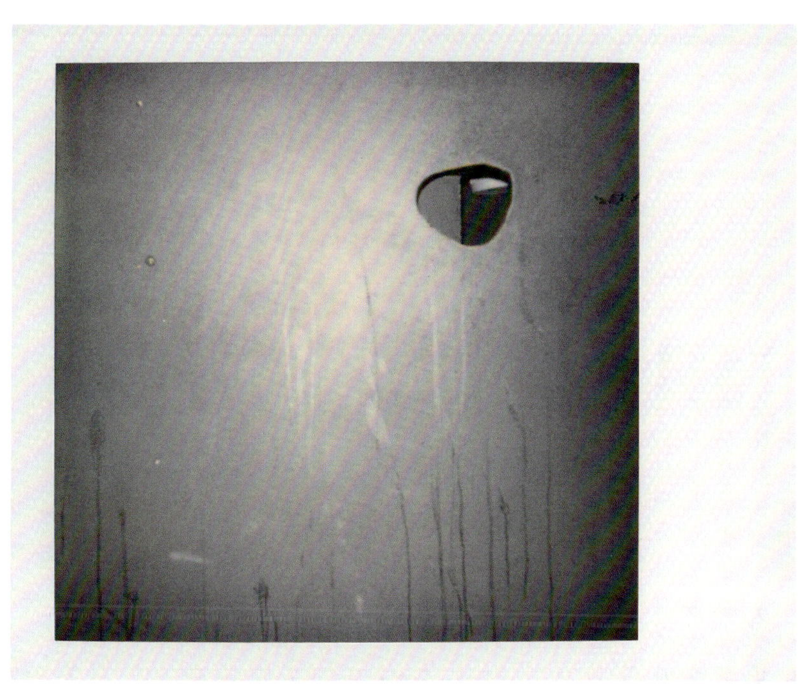

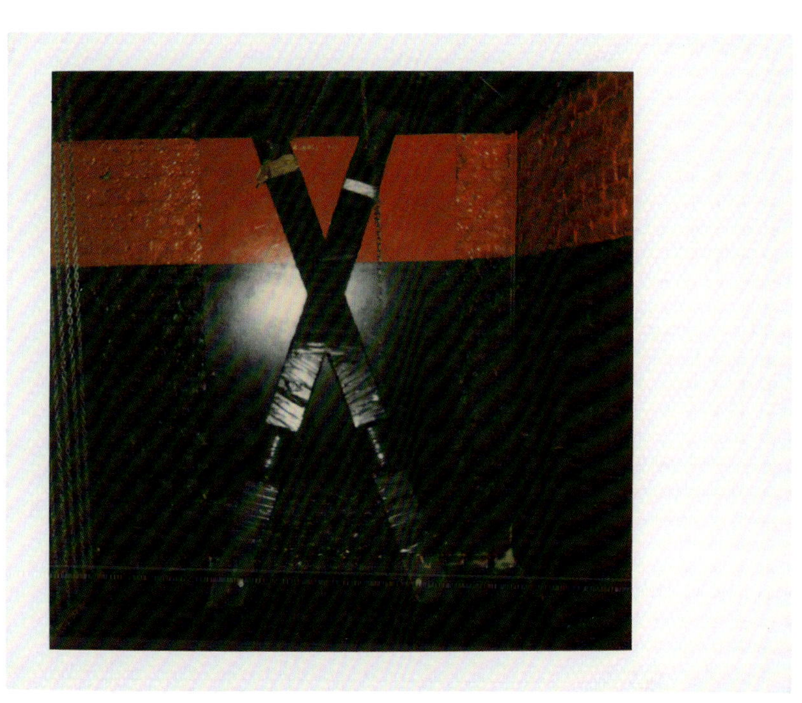

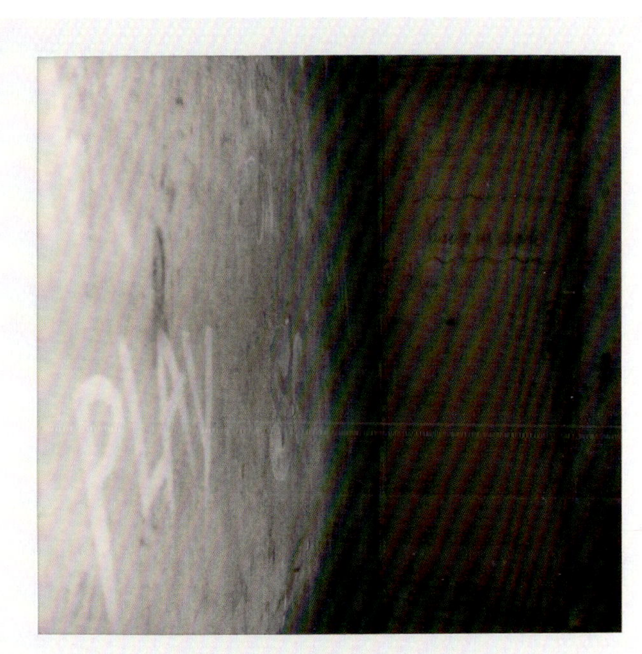

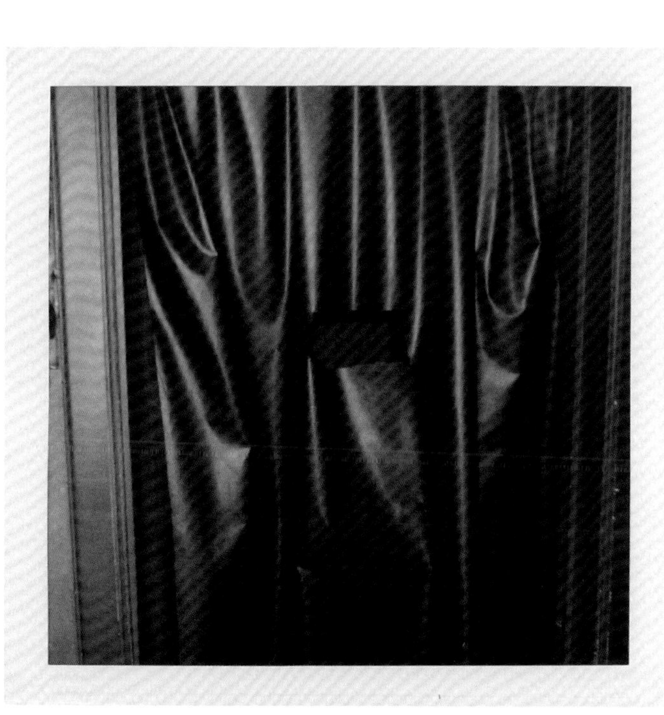

02084807 1
POLAROID 32

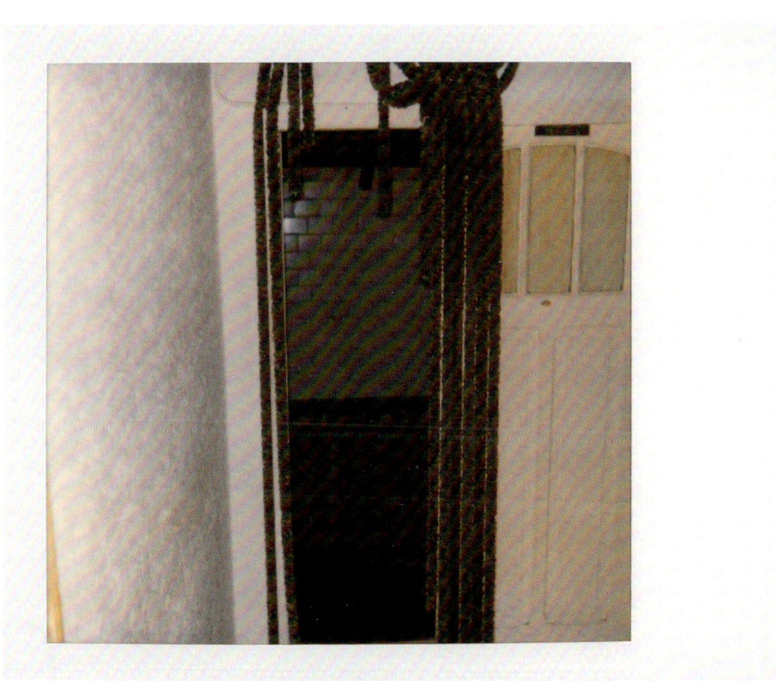

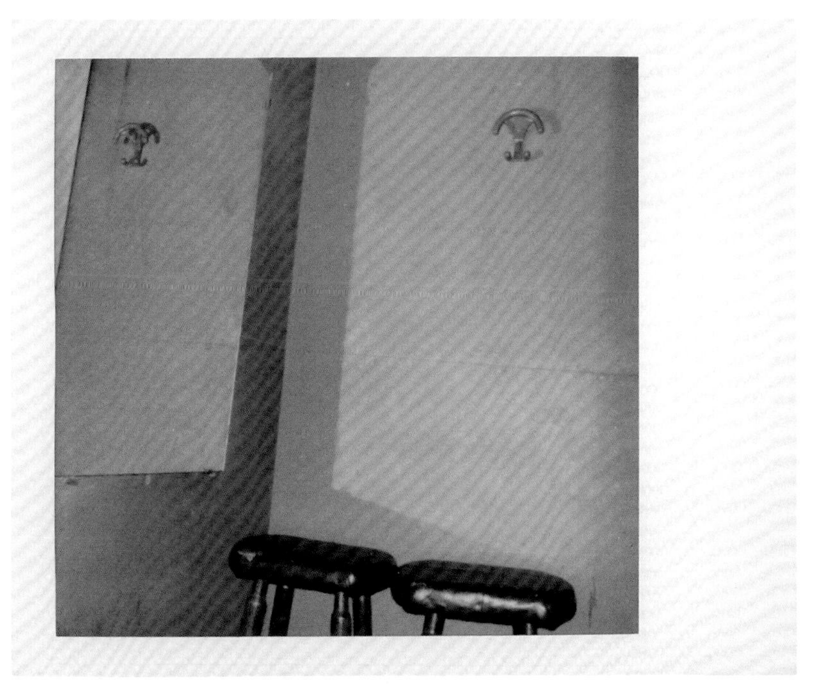

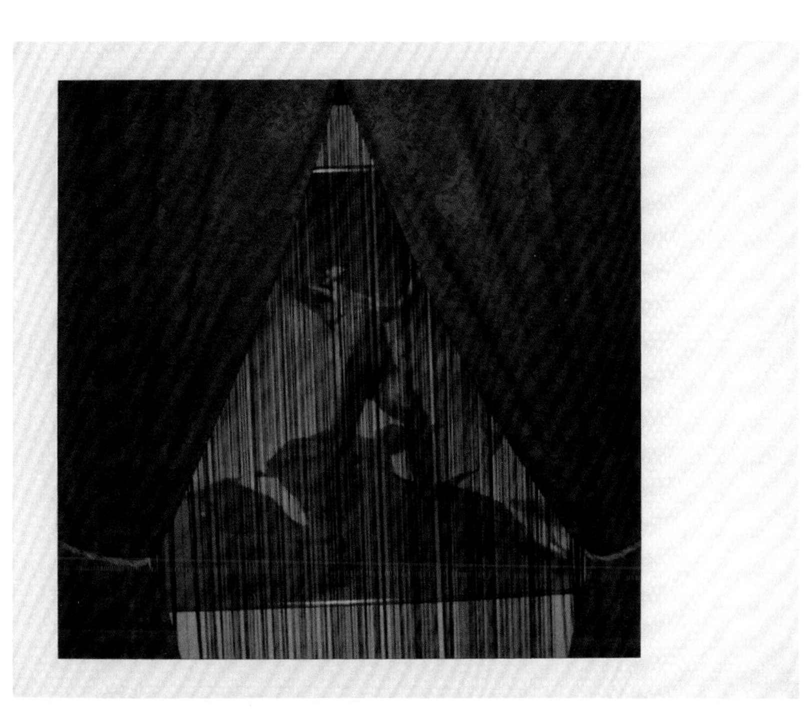

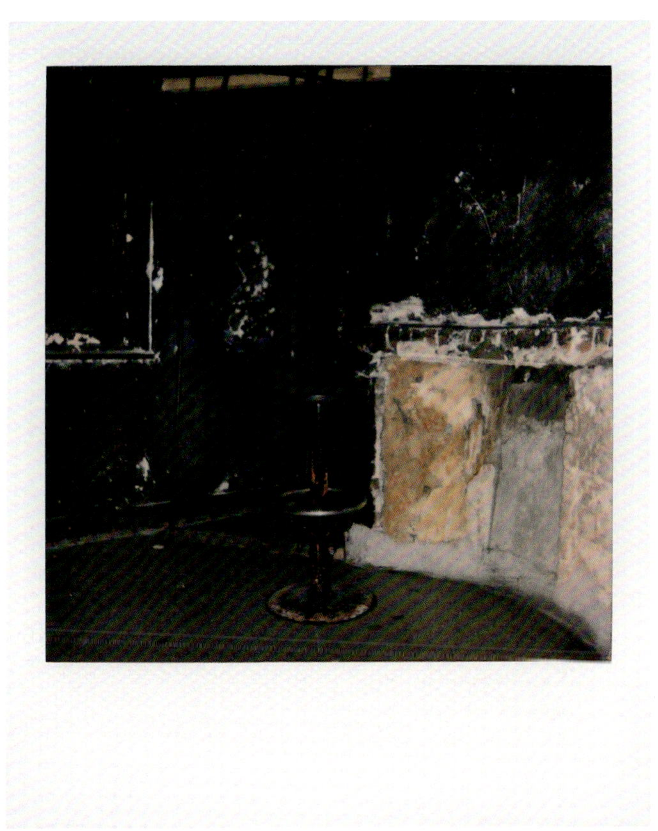

110731122
POLAROID

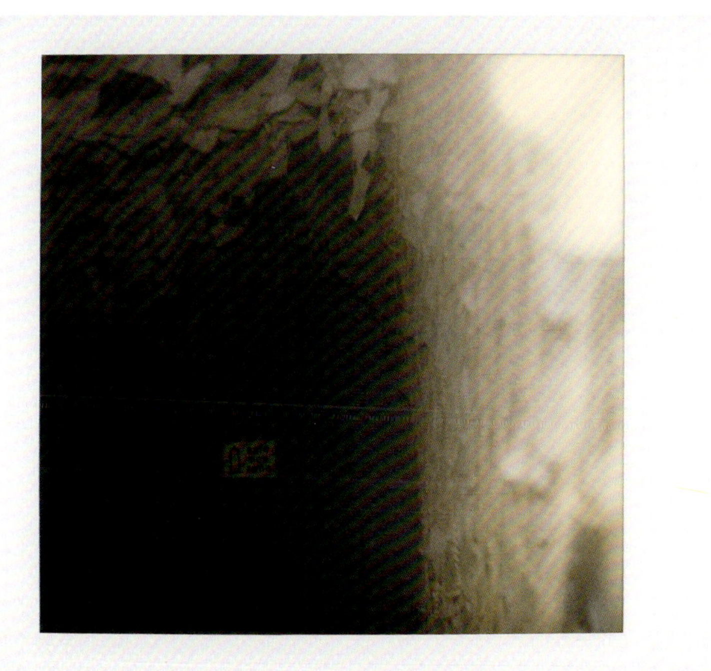

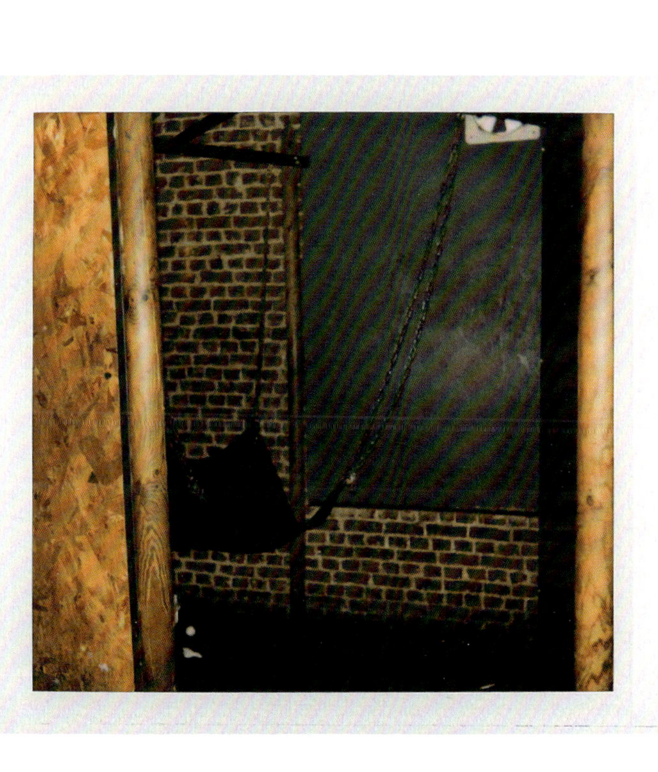

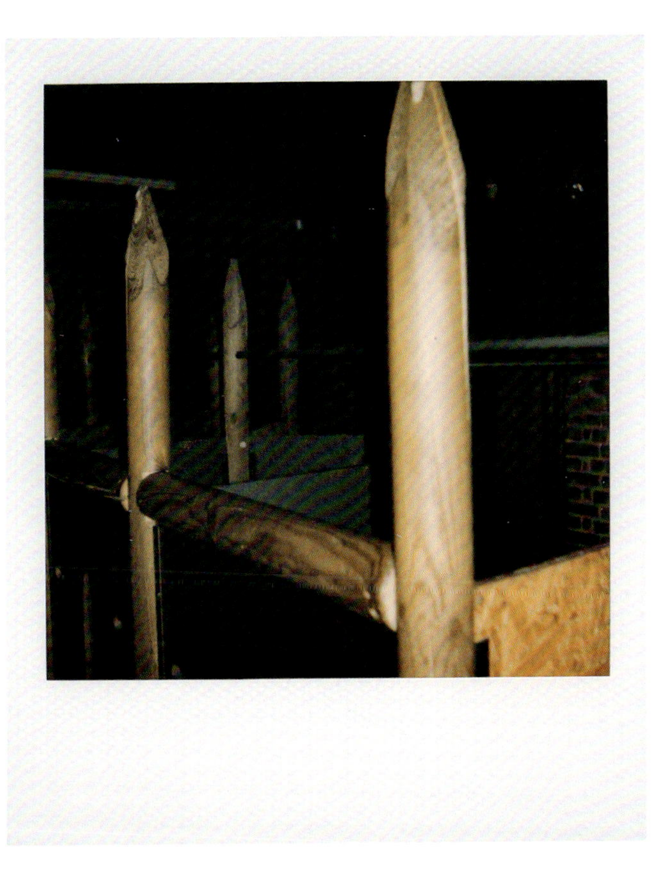

110731122
POLAROID 92

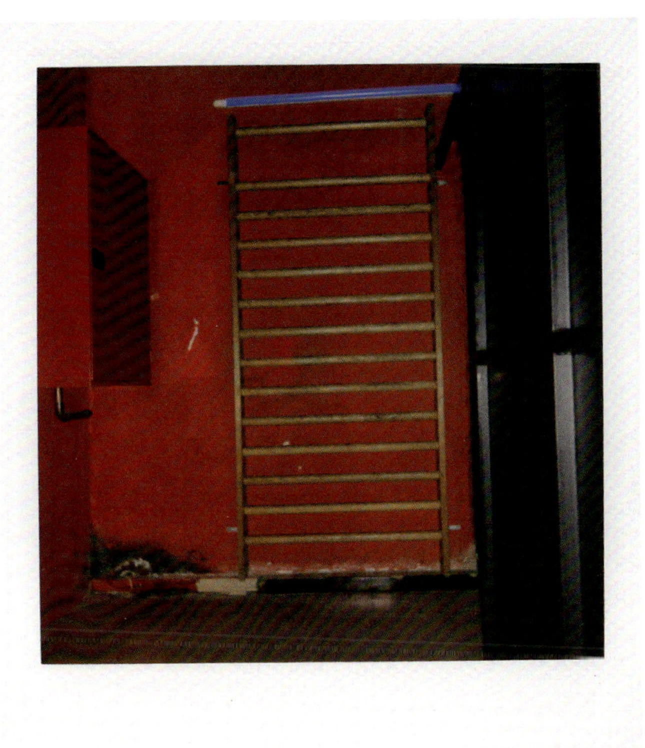

050744219
POLAROID 32

060747280
POLAROID 32

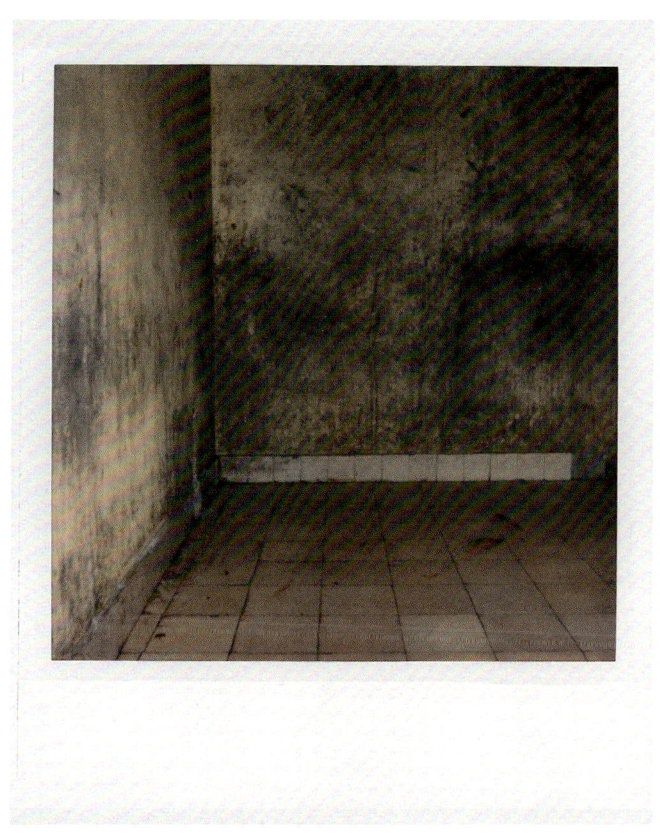

110731122
POLAROID 32

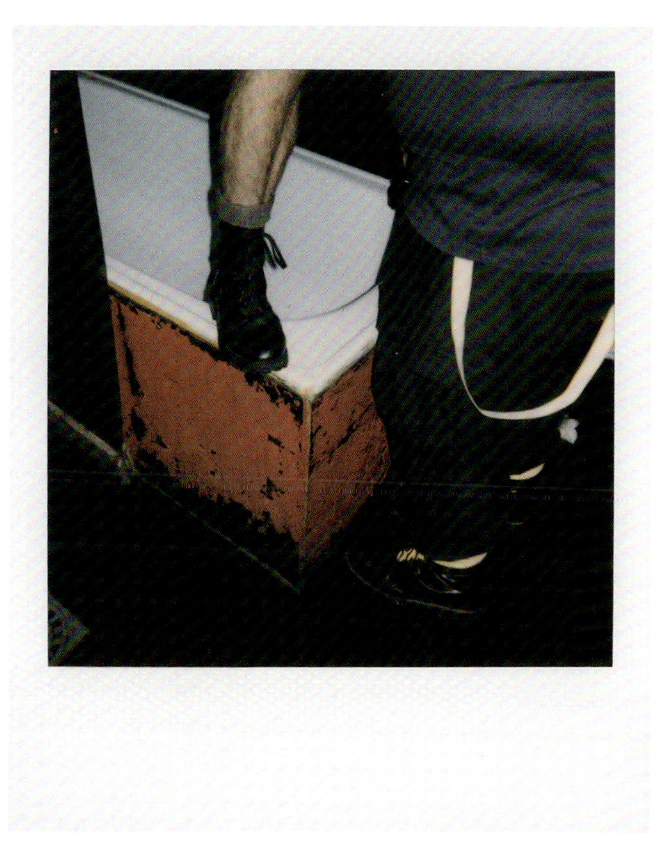

050744210
POLAROID 92

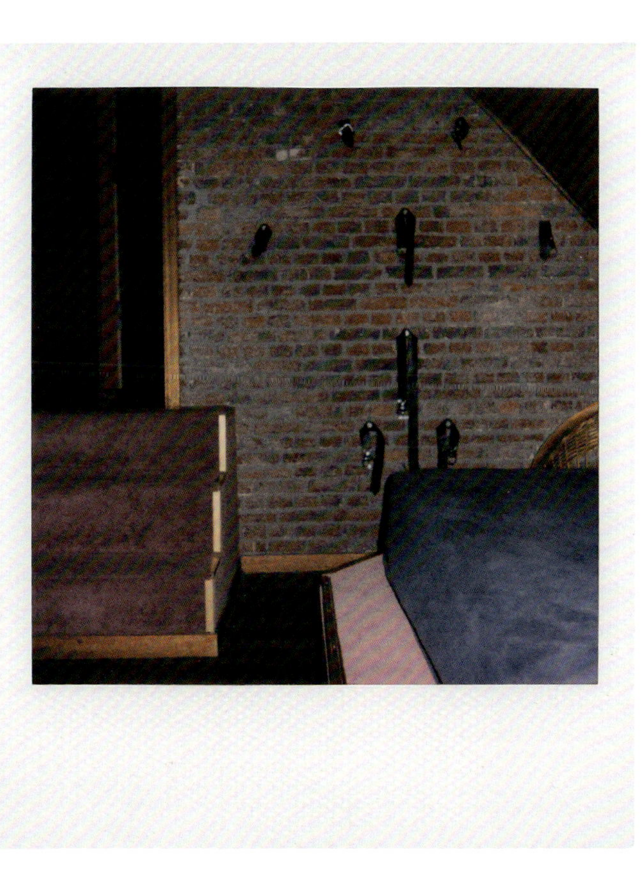

020848071
POLAROID 32

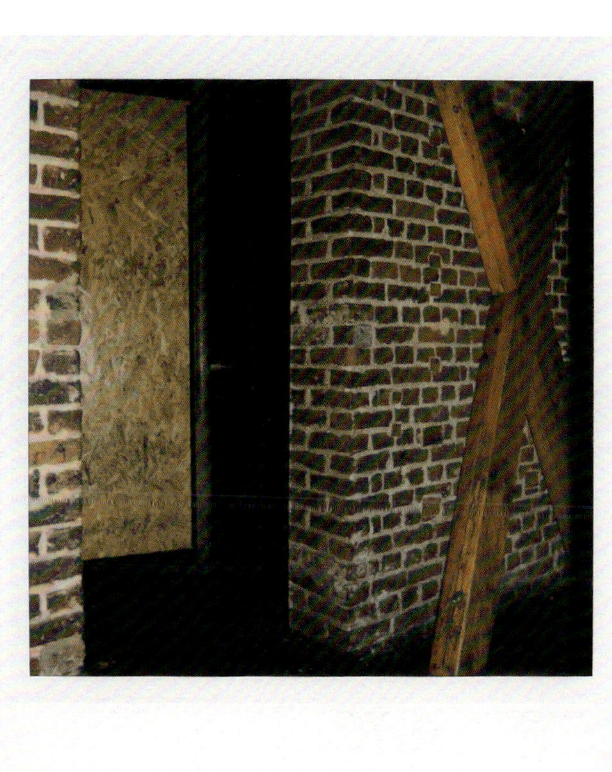

110731122
POLAROID 32
POLAROID©22

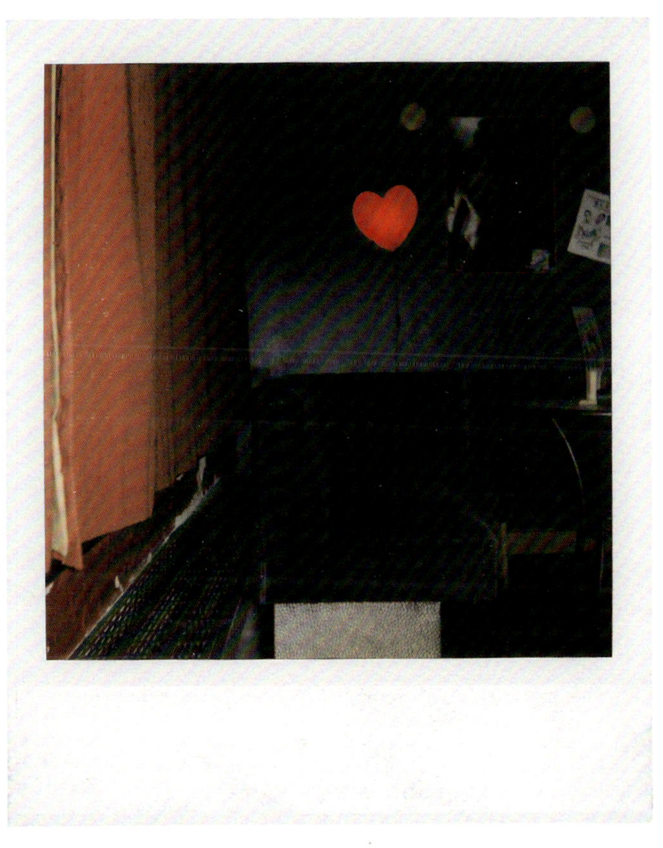

110731116
POLAROID

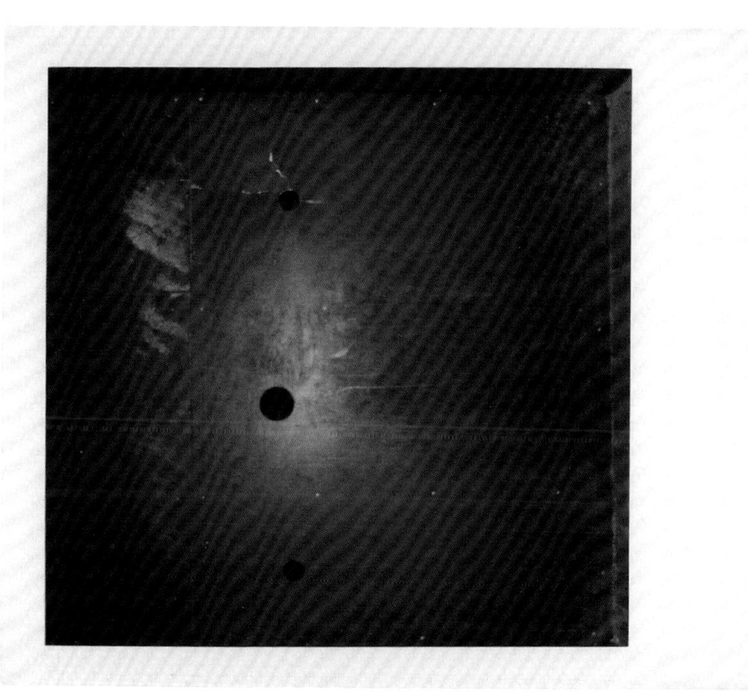

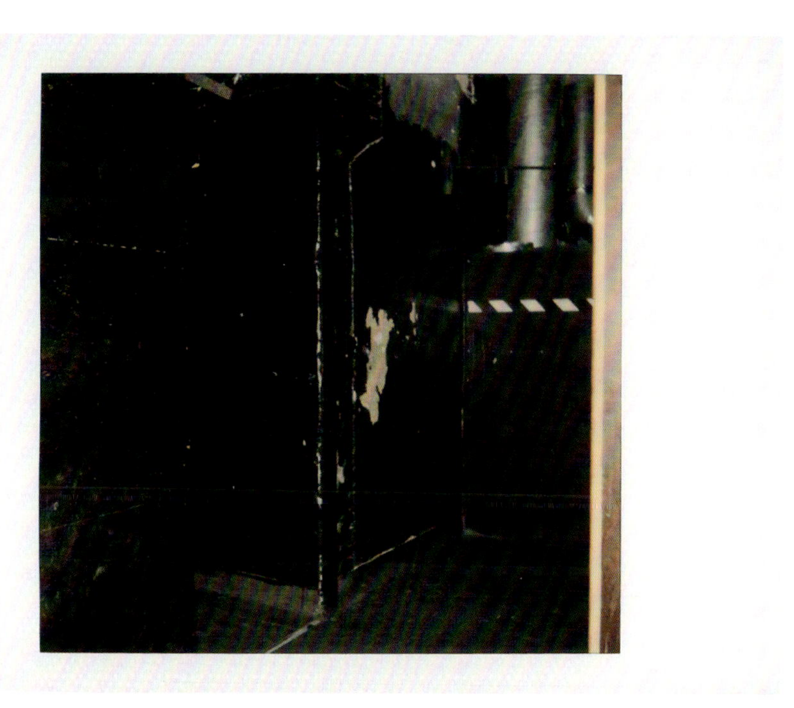

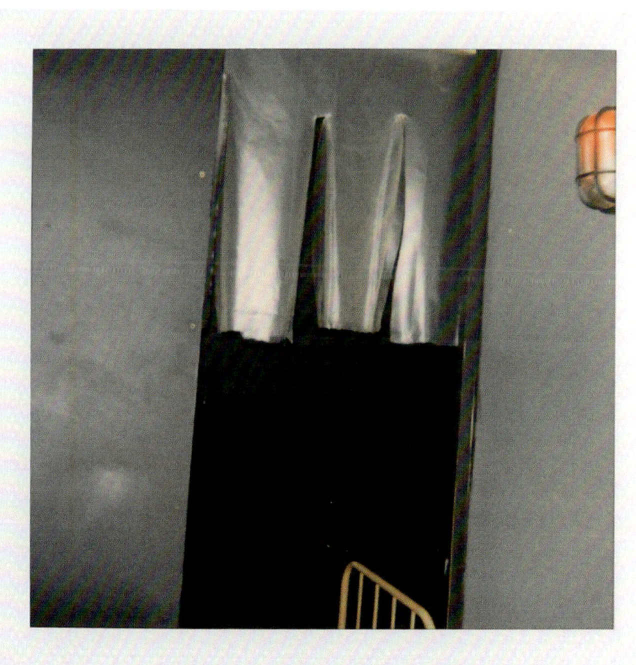

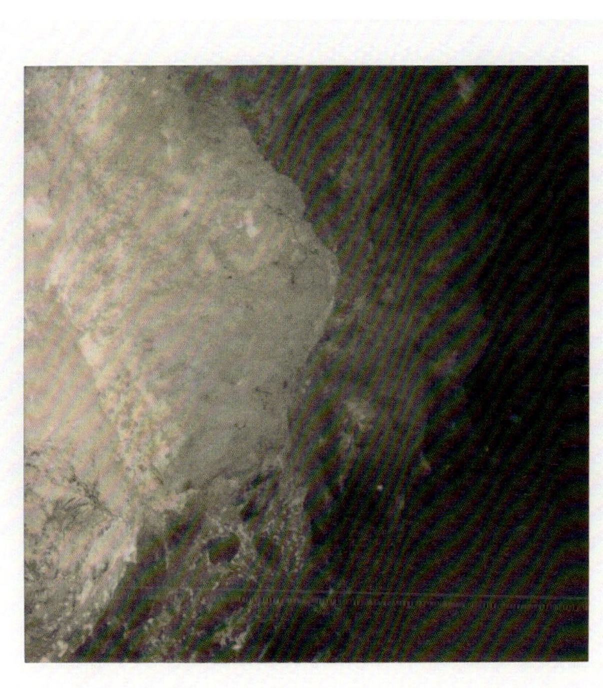

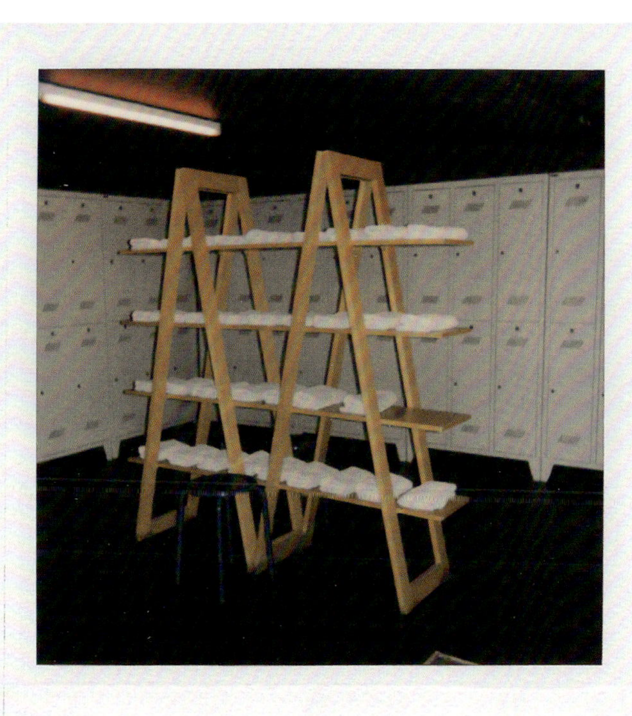

110731116
POLAROID 32
POLAROID®32

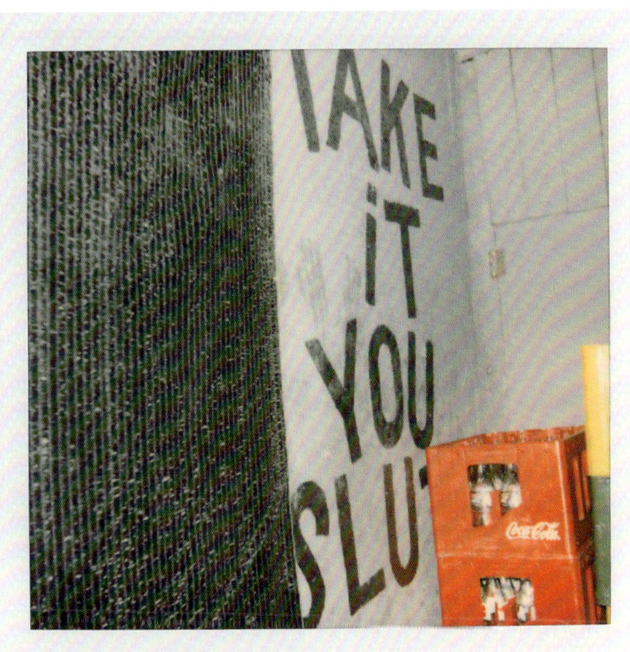
AKE
IT
YOU
SLU
Coca-Cola

PARADISE
OF
LUST

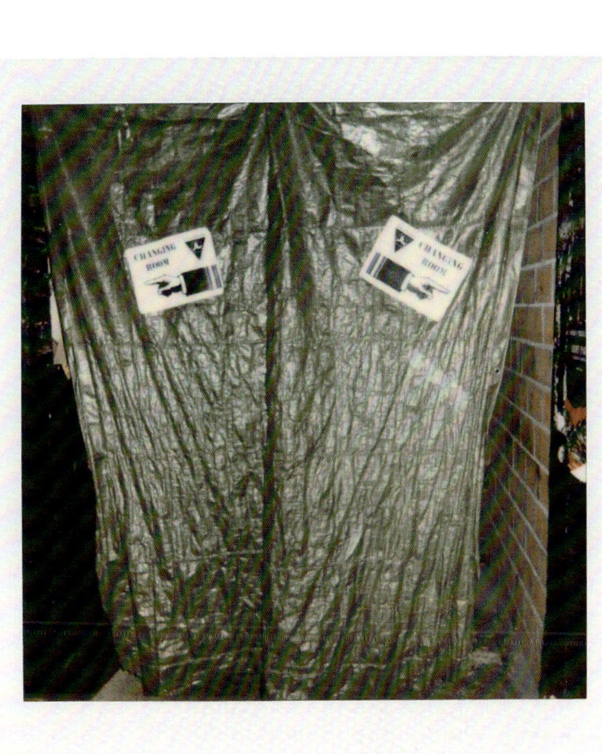
CHANGING
ROOM
CHANGING
ROOM

050744210   POLAROID 32